THE WORLD IS ROUND

Also by Nikky Finney

The Ringing Ear: Black Poets Lean South (edited anthology)

Heartwood (short-story collection)

On Wings Made of Gauze

Rice

Head Off & Split

NIKKY FINNEY

THE
WORLD
IS
ROUND

poems

Foreword by Kevin Quashie

TRIQUARTERLY BOOKS/NORTHWESTERN UNIVERSITY PRESS
EVANSTON, ILLINOIS

TriQuarterly Books
Northwestern University Press
www.nupress.northwestern.edu

Printed in the United States of America

10 9 8 7 6 5 4 3 2

Library of Congress Cataloging-in-Publication Data
Finney, Nikky.
    [Poems. Selections]
    The world is round : poems / Nikky Finney ; foreword by Kevin Quashie.
        p. cm.
    "First published in the United States in 2003 by InnerLight Publishing. This edition published in 2013 by TriQuarterly Books/Northwestern University Press by arrangement with Nikky Finney."
    ISBN 978-0-8101-5233-5 (pbk. : alk. paper)
    I. Quashie, Kevin Everod. II. Title.
PS3556.I53W67 2013
811.54—dc23   2013002126

For the tenderhearted insurgent
Lorraine Hansberry,
who "finished my thoughts"
long before I had them

You might think that a straight line is the shortest distance between two points

but a woman's eye can travel in a curved line when she needs to

see something and somebody is trying to keep her from seeing it,

her eye can travel in a curved line to get there and she will get there.

—MODJESKA SIMKINS

CONTENTS

Kevin Quashie

Nikky Finney's *The World Is Round* is a book to live by, a book that is full of sure magic. There is a rosary quality to the poetry here, as if it were prayer, as if its grace is revealed through repetition and patience, vulnerability and yearning . . . through engagement with the human interior.

The title poem opens the book and introduces a speaker who lays down the invocation—the idea that "the body can so / remember" things that the eyes cannot capture or the mind cannot make sense of. This assertion that memory not only resides in the body but is also cardinal is the heartbeat of the book. For Finney, memory itself is a body, a corpus of human experience and a source of counsel, if we deign to listen; in this regard, it is notable that the speaker in this poem is a yet-to-be-born child whose knowing is ancestral and cosmic. This is not romanticization but the deliberate work of engaging the past, "memorizing [one's self] back to life," as Finney terms it in "Mean Nina." (Interestingly, *Head Off & Split,* Finney's 2011 National Book Award–winning collection, opens with another young speaker, this one an errand girl, whose voice also invokes and counsels.)

The young-black-girl-as-oracle, one who is a student of the world.

What is celebrated in Finney's use of the human divine is the vernacular, the notion of a black manner of speaking that reflects wisdom which might be absent in formal speech. The vernacular is fascinated with language, with its capacity to express and deny, language as music and agency, language as breath escaping one body and entering another. For Finney, the language matters—not only the charisma of sounds but also the ethic: the language has to reach toward something meaningful.

You can see this commitment to the vernacular in the way Finney honors the power of the ordinary, the commonplace: for example, the book's study of what it is to be a daughter is both an intimate meditation on love and disaffection (a homophobic insult by a loved one) as well as a consideration of historical violence (racist church bombings). Nowhere is this marriage of the intimate and the social more evident than in the diction of "The Girlfriend's Train," where the speaker, a black woman poet, bonds with another black woman and considers the legacy of physical abuse. The poem's language moves from whispered terms to a vocabulary that is of the world ("cross-country," "latitudes," "longitudes," "equatorial line").

Finney never loses appreciation for the everyday humanity of her characters—the whimsy of her grandmother's shopping; the inner lives of young black men standing mournfully around a casket; the possibility of two firemen locked together in embrace, hanging perilously, their capacity to rescue linked to their willingness to need each other. This is her vernacular aesthetic and it is interested not just in the story but also in the storytelling; that is, these intimacies are narrated through exquisite engagement of poetic forms. For example, in "The Squatting Sun," the speaker tells of her own birth in a passage of remarkable rhythm and rhyme:

> Believed I had seen this daily drama before;
>
> the earth in morning-mother motion,
> the first bowl of earth-breath sipped,
>
> but never had I been asked
> inside the sun's womb so deep.

Here, the plethora of *d*'s and *m*'s repeated, the *d*'s and *p*'s in "sipped" and "deep" that pull these two words together, the phrasing "earth-breath," which is a revelation of both sound and meaning—all this music is assembled in holy couplet form. This evidence of the poetic is plentiful in the book. In "Afro-Gregorian Chant," Finney uses couplets again, but this time to create a steady clip, one line easing into the other, then breath, then two more lines in tandem, and so on. Or, in "Metallurgy," a poem for jazz maven Cassandra Wilson, Finney adopts a range of blues techniques: long vowel sounds, repetition with variation, signifying, and colorful phrasing.

And still, what is most absorbing about Finney's poems is the great care they take in showcasing that the inner life—the storehouse of our deepest human ambitions and neediness—is a habitat of agency. All activism is not to be surrendered to the exigencies of the social world; indeed, what is intimate is also political. In Finney's noticing, the human experience of being ravishing and being ravished is an apt idiom for deliberating the world. This sentiment is captured in the poem "The Making of Paper": dedicated to one of Finney's mentors, the late Toni Cade Bambara, the poem reflects on Bambara's request for some paper and a pencil in the last conversation between the two writers days before she died. What Finney does here is to morph the form of the rant into a tender-fierce meditation on what it means to love trees, love life, love black women, what it is to love writing and the work and word that black women do . . . what it means to live the way Bambara lived. It is a poem of maximum beauty, both in terms of the aesthetics and of the humanity it exudes.

The World Is Round evidences Nikky Finney's elegant vernacular and is a stunning achievement of verse. Finney has said that she wants to be "a poet who speaks / writes out of [her] deepest quietest place," and in this book we have just that: heirloom poems that speak through the human interior and that are lessons about ache and redemption.

The world is round indeed.

THE WORLD IS ROUND

The World Is Round: The Breast of
the Garment Measured

I began this side of life as infant photographer
focusing with the moving middle eye, the round
umbilical cord, where it melded into the body center
like a vacuum sucking in the sights.

Not with any eye but with skin did I see this,
do I remember now, the skin can so remember.

This picture that I first took of touch, here in the studio
body of birth, first photograph of feeling, anchored by
something other than the liquid albumen world where
I had lived from the first.

Something round, made of me and her and him.
Something akin to one large ballooning finger, here,
at the full lips of my belly's button where I could feel
the warmth of food; milky brown thick sugar passing

from her body's oven into my own whole-wheat capsule.
Too quick and the vacuum cord yanked, tugged me yet
another way and I twist-twirled around in my curved world,
falling back asleep, genuflected by her soft snaking octopus

arm. Only one hour old and I remember unlatching my eyes
to see the tiny incubating opening where I'd already lived
for a week, the warm stale air pouring in on me, not with my
mind but with full body camera do I remember this.

The perfect circular opening, round just like the cord,
round like the camera's eye, that I would one day accidentally

flutter inside, discovering silky stems of wildebeest poems
growing, sour sweet filigree weeds.

I always return to the glove of her body, the touch of her
chord to my middle, my middle to her chord, that opening
where I first fell in love with the breast of the garment, first
recognized what fit, though I could not yet safely wear it down

the daylight street. I can't show you any photographs of this
to prove what I'm telling you is true. I am remembering
this not with my mind but with my body, the body can so
remember what long ago left the accidental scene of the eye.

A woman has to be a daughter before she can be any kind of a woman.
If she doesn't have that in mind, if she doesn't know how to relate to
her ancestors, to her tribe, she is not good for much.

—TONI MORRISON

THE SQUATTING SUN

6:38, flying east, I witness birth,
pushing out of the blushing vaginal rim

like some wide cherry-dropped child.
All the colors that make red have come

to the only straight line on the earth.
Ghostly, I blink, my eyes tweak her nipples,

she releases and the head does not wait
for my awe.

I thought I knew what red looked like.
Believed I had seen this daily drama before;

the earth in morning-mother motion,
the first bowl of earth-breath sipped,

but never had I been asked
inside the sun's womb so deep.

What I see has so much to do
with the permission to look.

My egg-white eyes labor to midwife
this moment out all the way.

The baby day pushes clean,
a quarter rim of cherry-spilled earth

lands in a head-back wail
inside my ladling pupils,

the first rising brightness, its long
equatorial head bursts, then crests;

new life passed on
to a pan of waiting salted water.

CODA

We are four to a bed   So close our hips must come
with hinges   A ticking of brown family   Thrown
across the cotton and feather mattress of winter
Tucked   Deep inside the house my grandfather raised
up from the red earth straight into the woolly air

The black and white photograph isn't supposed
to predict the future   But my mother looks like my
unborn brother   And even at three I am different
My tiny Black girl eyes are a queer shade of green
At five my older brother stands there on the end
Already buttoned into my father's sense of place

We are so close in this cherry bed   Our lightly
touching hips must surely be hinged   Even the
children have them   Daddy has moved into place
next to Mama   Mama has moved in next to me
I am the only one awake   The only one with a wall
The whole house has fallen   The movie begins

Uncle Billy is just home from Vietnam   He is the
baby   In the ruddy speckled flicker he stands before
us with a new camera that the war bought him   I call
Uncle Billy *The Bonneville Man*   Just like Pop Leo
he can fix anything   Unlike him   He will only drive
a car if it's long and pretty

Thirty years later *The Bonneville Man* will die with
AIDS   Alone in another bed without hinges   A dozen
headlights polka dot the night screen wall   Every long
pretty car he ever owned drives by to pay its last

respects He snaps the picture of us all Horns blow
out in a scatter like blue Cadillac whales

We are a charm bracelet of a family bedding down for
the night We are in the outback of my mother's
country We have been laid flat for the sake of photography
The elder aborigines bump room-to-rafter watching us
amazed They whisper how much we resemble
early black-and-white TV.

By midnight more of us have joined more of us We
lop around the old four poster in a three-dimensional
ring like a Black family cutout doll We are joined
at the hip inside the old home house We have been hinged
together in a place pulled from the red ribs of ancient
Indian land Newberry

We are southern North American Africans When we
sleep together the rubbing of our bones makes for
a better crop Daddy's hip bone click-clacks into place
next to mama And a new brother seven years ten pounds
and eight ounces away from birth snuggles in next to me

The new tenant brother takes up space I thought was
all mine But Mama says not to move him She says
he's the last one She says he will always need more
of her The Silver Queen has already been harvested
The second reel begins

Somebody down the road passes a new baby over
a new grave freshly packed with seashells The simmering
dust is spinning off the blue corn silk The ochre wind
patty-cakes the glass until dawn I know better than to sing
along Mama would only turn and shush me Tell me
to stop playing with myself

This is why I always sleep by the wall   For company
So the movie will always have a screen   So the screen
will always have a witness   Now all I have to do is live
Big brother there on the end turns   I follow   Tumbling
in an arc of bones   Our hinges shift but never release
My feet and body begin to rise   I leave the floor without
warning   There is a white dog out in the woods howling

Pop Leo will shoot the white dog between the eyes tomorrow
then drag him back to the clearing near the arrowhead ground
He will never explain to me what madness is   And how we all
can go   I am the only one awake to see the end   For twenty years
something or someone will come and lift me to the ceiling and back
whenever it wishes   I will come to know this as brown girl levitation

The black snakes are tunneling under the hay in the barn
for warmth   I see the mice go still in terror at the long
dragon vessels nearing   They are born knowing they can
be swallowed whole   Like them I have wondered how long
it takes to die when you are eaten and made to watch

I am counting   Practicing my numbers   At the cow trough
that Pop built fifty years ago with heavy two-handed
pieces of limestone   The spigot is dripping nineteen drops
per minute   Eleven Twelve Fifteen   I work hard on learning
my numbers in case there is ever a test   The water drips all
night   Even though I used two hands to shut it off like I was told

Except for the howling of something white farther off
in the woods that has lost someone it resembles   I am
attached at the waist to my brothers by my mother
but I know I am free to fly   I am a lee little long legged girl
A southern mixture of red velvet rice and everything nice
I have no memory of winter as a child

A peacock is still something I have never seen before
But in two hours over breakfast Aunt Willa will lie
and say she has   Her sapphire words will glitter
like a tickling rain rolling off the curly tin roof of the barn
where Mama used to dry apples as a child   I will see
Aunt Willa's saucy words leave her mouth and hit
the frying air like that of a howling dog or a torpedoing snake

I will remember last spring at the county fair   When
Aunt Willa slithered toward us waving her turquoise
green tongue like a fan of exotic feathers   I do not
remember Daddy snoring back when we slept in this
warm ring of soft brown bones   Only now do I understand
that my random levitations and landings had everything to
do with four little girls from Birmingham and a bomb

The all-night rubbing of bones has turned the inside
tips of my fingers alabaster   The homemade cotton sheets
have been dusted on both sides with self-rising flour
I need help hearing the many broken whispers coming
through the walls up from the land   The dead skin
of my grandfather dropped for years into this dirt
like drum and bugle seed   Back then I believed bombs
came wrapped in Black churches

I always wanted a sister   Another girl to remember
the land   Another girl to help rewind the film back
onto the reel   Like shelves of brown Britannica
Pop Leo's arms always knew the answer to everything
No visible timepieces were ever kept in this house
that he built and she made   So we would never think
of leaving

Any minute I will smell her perfect fig biscuits being
pulled from the wood burning stove   He will pour

his black coffee out his cup and into his saucer   He will
drop his full Cherokee lips to the cool of the rim   He
will tilt himself back into a sip so long it will seem to pray
As the baby light comes inviting the day   I will hear him
wishing his throat was a mile long   Finally I am falling asleep

I am the only girl   I know the hinges we have worn
all night made of soft shell salmon bones will fall away
at the first shock of light   I know when the red rooster
finally steps it will be like High John the Conqueror
into the morning broom-swept yard

Only then   Will we unhook as a mule team from
the gingerbread night   Only then will we one by one
make our way into the icebox bathroom   Only then
in the face bowl will our image appear   Only then
will we wash our privates by ourselves

The New Medicine

Evening

I go home just to touch them.

Rent a car that is newer than my own
for the long drive there,
to be sure I arrive without delay.

First the purple Tennessee mountains
blur the wide hips of the windshield,
then the blue tar-heeled air
pours a southern smelling salt across my skin.

On the pedal my foot feels relentless,
I take the eight hours in one bite.
Before long the fat five hundred miles
eat all the sun out of the sky.

I am left a mere daughter
driving on sheer blacktop desire
to put my hands on them again.

That night I slump,
in a mother-daughter nest of repose,
repossessed once again
on her loud flowery couch.

My long fingers, delirious, spread,
lost in between her bare brown feet;
that underneath are sleeping jellyfish,
on top, squirming fiddler crabs.

She talks and I stare, the garden
of tiny lines around her mouth,
new rows, new rosebuds, in but a month.

I finger every bunion I can find,
lingering pumpkin prayers in between
the smooth hollows of a foot
belonging to us both.

I never drive home to see them,
never arrive anxious to twist toward
their echoing laughter,
I travel mile after mile just to touch them.

Morning

I could find him in my sleep if I had to
but I only have to push the screen
to enter my father's morning territory.

One tiny acre of back porch land
where he always sits in the last
of the earth's night melanin.

He and his companion cigarettes have spent
fifty years of mornings together,
his sweet morning raspiness as predictable
as Sunday morning salmon and grits.

My fingers move like a honeyed light
for the back of his head. I move in behind his chair,
reach-drape my arms across his chest.
Bending, I berth his cheek with mine.

Our father-daughter chin hairs
yin yang graze, like two of the same kind
of cat. My hands fold, braid out across his chest,
in an old sweetgrass weave, that if unraveled
would spill the story: how we own each other's heart.

I lean back into the wall, one hand falls down loose
across his neck bone, the other takes to his jaw and
stays, rubbing his prickly chin there until the sun
brilliantly permissions me to go.

Twilight

I go home just to touch them.

Their black crystal lives genie rub against me,
polishing. Long before reports appeared of touch
being the new medicine of the new millennium.

Before touch suddenly became in and all the rage,
moving in beside echinacea and New Age healing.
Before they invested millions in New England clinical trials,
needing to study it all up close.

Before handing puppies to prisoners as salvation
and kittens to old folks in nursing homes. Before telephone
commercials sold everyone on the many intrinsic benefits
of it and long distance.

By camel, bus, train, or foot; I traveled.
My empty hands begging, breathless,
twin compasses spinning before me
for the unpanned gold of their skin.

For the oldest brother's patty-cake back hug,
for the youngest brother's full lip kiss,
for my grandmother's forward bent body
pushed snug into my waist.

So snug, that days later, I find her still there.
In the bog of the bathroom mirror, pushed tight,
her silhouette still floating, still cameo-ed
just above my navel.

I never drive to see them. Never drive to
listen, as they whisper, shout out my name.
But I will do anything just to touch them.

My hands, whenever they are near, renamed
Cassiopeia, twin fraternal lanterns of every
seafaring daughter, clothed in gauzy winding
memory paper, she always pointing out to me
the copper coordinates of wherever they may be.

LOBENGULA: HER WALL-BOUND CHILD

Behind my side of the headboard
my son sleeps with me,
both eyes frozen open
all through the night.

When I make queen-size love
in a woman's pot of heat,
or dream a fetal curl around
a word, frenzied to finalize a line,
his glass-housed body
tap-taps against the wall.

His brown ocean face
becomes a dandelion tree.
I blow him around
with my eyes,
seeds fly between us.

We scandalize the room,
his tiny invisible voice
always the pollinating one,
Mommy, you're trying too hard again.

Each time he opens his floating
mouth a black bunched web
of his boyish silk skates across
the air, my new mother's netting
stretches out to hold, fragile
as ten teacups full of a baby's
first breath.

Lobengula has my ropey hair,
my spacey teeth, my love for precision,
but wears someone else's tentative smile,
looking something but nothing like me,
all at once.

He is a found-child, in an airport
gift shop in Kingston, covered in island
sugarcane dust then mailed to me
duty-free way back across the water.

He arrived with the gift card still tied to his
framed wrists. A name tag whispering
on a summer train child on the move between families,
And you thought you'd never have a son. Love, Lorna

He is all the brown face boy
I will ever have.
All I will ever nail
Jesus-high into a birth wall.

I have missed ever knowing him,
missed marking his height off on
the kitchen wall, missed lip kissing
my morning worry into the mitt of his hand
or shining my nose into his sleeping
high school breath in search of homemade
wine, guzzled he finally confesses,
in the bus lot between state championship quarters.

Who is that?
Wanderers to the bedroom always want to know.
That is my son. He lives behind me where I sleep. He is a wall-bound child.
What is a wall-bound child? And when did you have one?
The wanderers push.

It means if he leaves the air in this room he will die without me.
But he is too big to still sleep with his mother. What will people say?
They will say that I am unfit to have a son that can never leave his mother's room.

(But they will be so wrong.)

MEAN NINA

Lying there in state when I arrive is Great-Aunt Nina.

Nina of the pear gum trees, of the old old ways,
seamstress of flowers so fine, thread laid to silken
seed, inside the eyelids of raw cotton.

Nina Davenport could sew the wing back on a butterfly,
make them rise, cocoon, bloom again. On every arm
of every chair in the old home house, her linen
butterflies fluttered, her needles pursed a power.

Lying there now is mean Aunt Nina, who won't die.

Nina, the general. Sergeant maiden of the farm,
distributor of all good backbreaking work within
a five-mile radius. Mean Nina, devoted sister of Daisy,
the sweet. I lift the sheet to see what lies left of her.
What shakes out is one long-as-me crooked trembling bone.

She is without clothes from the waist down.
The diaper stamped Large Adult. A middle passage
insignia. My eyes run headlong into a summer afternoon
shower. Still wet, they whisper to her Jesus, "Don't you
keep me here this long."

I cover back up her protruding pelvic bone that was
once her Black woman's saucy hip. I keep my hand
on her posting family messages through my fingers
all along her body board.

They never touch her here. They change her diaper when
they please, their latex hands rake her long Indian hair,
with what should be saved for mules, archaeological digs.

I look inside her table drawer. The soft brush that Mama
brought Thanksgiving Day is gone, disappeared with all
the other nice things. I turn to stampede the office again,
like all the other times before.

I want to know how they can steal from a woman
who won't die, but her eyes fall on me like a shaft,
"Don't child, you get to go and I get to stay. You don't
know the half of mean when nothing but your mind
can leave the room."

Aunt Nina goes on to tell me there is good news. She insists
that I take word of it back to family. "I am no longer the
meanest woman in the world." We smile. She goes on.
"The new night nurse, the one called Little Mary, has now
won the crown." Little Mary, who every time I walk in,
never looks me in my eye.

Every time Mary comes into the room Aunt Nina stops
whatever she is saying, and turns her voice into a needle
or a knife, searching for the jugular of Little Mary's ear,
and pushes: *One day you will be old. You will. I won't
be around to see it but word will come.*

All day Aunt Nina thinks and stares. Rolled up fetal, unable
to go anywhere except in her head. Every day staring down
the wall as it grows from dark to light. No corn to shuck. Page
to turn. Thread end to lick.

She remembers now with worry how mean to everyone she was.
"Mean Nina," Mama and the rest of us would whisper every time

our car pulled into her yard, just before walking into her house
of linen butterflies and fresh pole beans.

That was when Nina Davenport could walk away from you
with great purpose. When everybody thought she would
just die easy, like the rest of us. Teacher. Farmer. Spinster.
She surprised everybody and married a short man once.

The land needed a man's back for a season and all the other
hired hands had escaped away one night or another. Eventually,
he would flee too. The night before he ran the new pastor had
just preached, "Meanness do not wear down," his hand pummeling
the gospel plow—"meanness," he swore, "lasts longer than plastic."

I grew up scared of Nina Davenport. But that was before, when I
believed she would just die regular. Back then I would fly out of
her way like a biddy in a barnyard too close to a boot. Now that she
is flat on her side, buckshot as a red fox, I stand as close as I can,
amazed that something, finally, has laid her meanness down.

On the outside Nina Davenport is helpless. But on the inside she is
whole. Little Mary hates Aunt Nina. She knows her body is gone
but doesn't know her mind is perfect. Nina Davenport won't just go
on and go, like the other ones that give up easy, die quick.

On Sundays Aunt Nina prays out loud for lightning to come,
to strike Mary down. She clarifies that this is not further evidence
of her meanness, just everlasting belief in the power of prayer.
Whenever Mary enters the room she walks right over to the window
first thing and closes the drapes.

Aunt Nina's forty-year teacher's pension pays the bill each
month. She doesn't care about the money going up like
smoke, only about the giving up, of Mary winning. She says
her bones are all iron and castor oil now. She says when we

first left her in this place she declared war. She says this proud,
like a soldier cleaning her gun between battles.

When I stand there beside her she recites Robert Frost,
summons the battle of Fort Sumter, remembers the capitals
of all the states. She asks me to sing them back to her. I do.
I know she is memorizing herself back to life.

She mumbles out recipes that won't work without freshly
churned butter, the twenty-nine places on her five hundred
acres where she planted heirloom pears that still pop out
every July, still fall to the red ground, her hands no longer caramel
cupped doilies, saving them from the rabid ground worms.

Then there are all the names, of all the neighbors come
and gone. Then, every year of every flood and which
house it took down what river. Then, which summer
the tornado laid everybody down in the snake ditch
like pine board, one crooked row of outstretched prayers,
a family of drenched sin rising finger first to the crazy sky.

Her mind perfect,
her body dead.

Here at the end she only wants two things. She asks if I've
remembered to bring them. I reach into the bag and sit them
on the nightstand. Aunt Nina strains her eyes to see.

I tear off the wrapper. I hold it out for her long inspection.
She inhales, sighs, is her usual disappointed. "It used to smell
meaner than that." She runs her fingers across the silky
sunken word, LIFEBUOY.

I warm the face cloth and slowly wash around her neck, eye
sockets, temple. She quivers when I touch inside her ears
but does not turn away. Her nose widens, smelling salvation,

then her eyes close remembering something private, something
I can never ever know.

I tell myself only this old soap and ninety years of meanness
can do this to a woman. Make her feel something so old,
so new, here at the end. I dry her off easy with the good
towel that Mama gave me, then uncap the blue top from the
white opaque jar.

She bends her nose my way to test, then closes her eyes while
the whole world turns sepia. The Pond's cold cream covers my
two pointing fingers like an old woman's icing. Her skin dines.
I know that what I bring her in my paper sack is only her second
pleasure; the way she remembers how not to die.

She turns her face up to me just before I finish.
I rub around her tinted eyes again before I go. I know
I am tending to the beveled glass of a razed cathedral.
She touches my arm to whisper, "I guess I got to pay
for all them mean days?"

I lie. I say, "No ma'am."

THE RUNNING OF THE BULLS

Buy all the land you can buy while you can. So you never have to work for a white man. Dickman already did that. Already hit him for you too.
—LEO H. DAVENPORT, MY GRANDFATHER

After slavery there were other chains.
The South still rounded up Black men

who wouldn't look the other way,
drop eyes or chin,

pass or step aside,
be cheated.

Men who saw red every day,
infrared patches glaring off

the white shirts of white men.
Black men who raised families first

then their scale of justice fists,
run out of the South

into the mist of the North.
Uncle Dickman (with his blue-eyed self)

saw red every day
and finally oceaned a white man's face into it,

for cheating him of hard-earned wages.
Uncle Dickman, strapped North, before sundown

underneath the belly
of a wagonload of hogs.

For fifty years Granddaddy's eyes lusted for land,
the morning paper; a hunter's inky den,

afterwards, his daily bread of sermon sliced
in even loaves garnished on the sides

of oven-warmed Sunday plates.

ELEPHANTINE

i

I rode the head of an elephant
around and around
the dime store parking lot,
my long colored legs
dug in behind
his huge floating ears.

His body hair prickly,
a carpet of black straight pins
sticking me in the soft
sockets of my skin.
The chain around his wide foot
scraping the concrete,
both of us trembling
to not be there.

I was seven,
the man below smiling,
his long tall stick
writhing in the air
a charming snake.
Mommy said
I should ride the elephant
because traveling shows
didn't come our way often
and might never again.

> *You'll always remember this,*
>   she promised.

28

The elephant shuffled beneath me,
his body crying as loud for home
as mine for ground.

This is all that remains
of a girl of seven,
everything else shattered now
broken into fragments
gone the way of pigtails,
presidential assassinations,
and Black Power movements.

ii

Tonight on the news:
South African baby elephants
stripped of their mothers
and acacia trees,
waiting to be shipped
to more circuses and zoos.

Shackled just above their new knees,
hobbling about in tiny pens
until feet suddenly begin to move
like the fins of a huge land fish,
something with a longer snout,
something acaciaed has just
crossed their inner eye.

Without warning one of them
pushes away from the fence,
flings her ton of memory into the air,
and tries to catch it with her trunk;
burning to feel it again
what it's like to be elephant.

She bolts straight across
my dime store parking lot,
her diamond cut ears flap and flail,
the hairy straight pins prick,

I swat the back
of seven-year-old legs,
You'll always remember this
comes across my headset,
I cup my ears
as she hits the electric wire.

THE UNDERSEA WORLD OF JACQUES COUSTEAU

The summer of '63
and I am only one Black girl
who belongs to the South.

A privileged one
who gets to walk to church
then mosey back home alive
without the pin of a bomb
clasped in my hair.

I am tiger-eyed and sandy-haired
and never afraid to jump
in the deep end of the city pool.

Men of all colors are being shot
like ducks on the wall
of America's country fair.

And the small eyes in my mama's house
are not allowed to watch TV news
but from the first we are encouraged to swim.

My grandmother tells me that in every
body of water deep enough to drown
there are people we know. She says
I should learn to swim, eyes open.

My fried bologna sandwich
has been eaten in the round.
A glass of Nestlé's chocolate milk
is one-half empty. I am spooning

leftover chocolate sludge up
from the bottom into my mouth
like sand candy.

My library books have been read;
they sit inside a Piggly Wiggly bag
rocking on the back door, waiting
to be returned.

I know I only have twenty-eight minutes
before Mama pulls into the yard,
sees me idle, leaps into her arias:

Why haven't you finished?
How was your spelling bee today?
Come help me with these beans.
Remember, I'll have no lazy daughter
living in this house.

I slide over to the wide glass box
that sits just off the floor,
one side houses Daddy's jazz records
the other says RCA Victor.
I turn the knob even though
there's not enough time.

My ears cup around the driveway,
my fingers go right to work,
it takes a long time for the light
to magically burst into form.

I push away, dragging my long body
back across the linoleum.
All my life I've been warned
about being too close to things.

But even at this young age I realize
I am five parts water, three parts magnet,
and positively electrical
about the things that matter most.

The screen door is closed,
the wooden one open,
it's not supposed to be
but I like things unshut.
I can see the yard,
hear Mama's Buick coming,
the soprano crickets are early.

A neighbor passes easy through
the hole in the back fence,
raising his right arm in a half wave
he moves through our part into his,
he doesn't stop to notice who is
or who is not inside.
Living or dead he understands
someone is there.
This is the kind of respect
I grew up with.

My head turns back to the RCA Victor.
A man comes into view,
pushed there by all the waves.

He is sitting on the edge of a boat
named *Calypso.* I like the name.
He looks like some kind of hybrid fish
or tired seabird. I angle my head sideways,
I have never seen a white man like him before.

It is 1963 and I am only one Black girl
from the South. One thing is for certain;
I do not trust white men.

I know them as creatures
who throw smoking things,
hide their many hands, disappear
out of sight.

A salty sea air is coming through
the old RCA Victor now. I inhale,
sit up straight, forgetting about Mama
and the time.

He is there again, an old white man
in a tiny red bathing suit no bigger
than a smile. There is something
watery about him that makes me
not turn away.

I laugh at his tiny bathing suit,
notice his arms moving like propellers.
He is dramatic.

I try out his language. A Black girl
from the waters of South Carolina
suddenly speaking a salty French.

I repeat the words as if I'd said them
all my life. English appears down low
on the screen.

Every living thing needs water.

The interviewer explains
the seabird man's invention
and what a special moment
this is for the world.

We are about to go beneath,
to a place most have never seen before,
the Aqua-Lung, a diving saucer machine
will take us there. I like seeing things
that no one has ever seen before.

I ignore everything that has ever
been told to me about being too close
to things electric and move in.
I am inches away from a screen of waves.

He takes one backward splash
that is so close that I reach and wipe my face.
Soon we are inside its belly moving along
wondrous spidery walls.

The old man's eyes swim soft and wild
behind a glass mask. I try out the words
of my newest language:

étoile de mer
tortue de mer
corail
oursin
algue

I disobey the haunting of southern
Black girl routines and practice
his every word,

Bienvenue dans l'océan Atlantique.

We are speaking the same language now,
a dialect of water and salt.
I am frozen on his wavy channel,
the seawater in me swelling.

I am more Atlantic than anything,
having been born there, right between
its lips, still having people, four-hundred-
year-old cousins, never met, still there.

I do not yet know who this man
wearing two smiles is. He is so slight,
so awkward, so chalky white, so comforted
by my sea.

We have nothing in common except this
wet salty place where suddenly I realize
we both are from.

I think to myself: What if tomorrow,
on their way to work, all the white men
in the world drop themselves over
the sides of their boats,
I might get to know them too.

Mama has pulled the Buick all the way in,
and cut its trembling engine. I reach and turn
off the RCA Victor, before he pulls himself
all the way out of the water.

My fear: once out of the sea, he will be
just another white man rising from the depths,
a land creature once again able to hurl
sizzling rocks and words, fire his gun,
then hide his hand so well. These ones,

their faces always cloaked in the
catastrophic language of shoot first,
divide, and conquer.

Cousteau pulled me into the old water,
took me to see his violent peaceful planet.
He as fragile as it. We as vulnerable
as anything new.

There, in the old water, where always I felt
safe, safer than on any bloody land
ever walked, beneath the Confederate flag
of South Carolina in 1963.

"Ain't Too Proud to Beg"

—THE TEMPTATIONS, 1966

Ho Chi Minh
and my father
chain-smoked
Salem cigarettes
all their lives.

I am my father's
manifesto.
His little red book
begging him to stop.

HURRICANE BEULAH

Chapter One: Counting Straws

My grandmother is here visiting. This morning while she was
still asleep on her back I crept up close and counted them
all again. I've been studying Beulah Davenport's chin hairs
for years now, hoping to know something about her powers.
She has nineteen chin hairs which are sometimes there and some-
times not. I stand in the doorway watching her in the bath-
room mirror surrounded by Pop Leo's things; his razor and
cup always on the side of the face bowl. Eventually, she will
smooth pearl-white lather down around her chin. Suddenly
she is a tiny Black woman Santa, a caramel colored *I Love
Lucy* in classic pose, all in one. I like to watch as her ninety-nine-
year-old hands move sideways across and under the belly
of her barely wrinkled face. She does not see me leaning
into the door wishing she wouldn't shave away her golden
woman chin straw. *This is my research material!* I want to
scream. She does not know that I believe these hairs hold
the key to all her powers. She never sees me counting, pull-
ing, on the tiny hairs beneath my own chin, wondering
when, when can I count on being just like her?

Chapter Two: The Shopping Spree

-I-

*This morning at breakfast we had an argument about putting the
cans and bottles into the recycle bin instead of the trash can.* She
refuses to do it. I keep going behind her retrieving the shiny
see-through things from the garbage. Yesterday she told me
that only white folks save bottles and cans. She says Black

folks save the earth just by getting up in the morning and deciding to go on one more day. *Yes ma'am,* I answered. I tell her I want to buy her something new for her 100th birthday. She says there is nothing new under the sun. I ask her will she go to the mall with me to help me find it. She cuts off my sentence as soon as she hears the word *mall.* She says in her most amazed voice that she just heard on the radio that it's Senior Citizens' Day at the Salvation Army thrift store. She says, *Can you believe it, everything with blue and yellow tags is 50% off!* Already she is reaching for her pocketbook and slipping it on her arm and handing me my keys that I do not remember asking her for.

-2-

I am sitting at a four-dollar desk at the Southside Salvation Army thrift store biding my time by writing poetry. It is badly stained and wobbly, not the poetry I hope, but the desk. Every now and then somebody walks by and kicks the legs of it like it is a car they might want to take home. Just in the nick of time, I manage to raise my writing hand in the air, then wait for the table to stop shaking, as they decide whether they want it or not. Eventually, I go back to my writing. I've only had to change tables three times. Every now and then I look up from my writing to find my grandmother teetering down a row of color-coordinated clothes. She is moving down row seven now like an old loggerhead trying to decide where best to lay her eggs. She is holding on to her walker, which along with her hearing aid she hates to use in public. At the same time she is pushing a rickety shopping cart. I don't know how she is doing both these things at the same time but she is. She is definitely one part magic. Every time I ask her does she need my help she sucks her teeth real loud and moves on up the aisle away from me, blues singing something about, "Don't treat me like I'm old, treat me like I can be recycled, remember."

40

-3-

She is up in aisle seven carefully putting two- and three-dollar
dresses into her push basket. Some of them I can see are
expensive tweed and gabardine suits that I imagine rich ladies
gained weight and outgrew. Some of them, I imagine, those
same rich ladies might have worn up until their last day on earth.
I imagine their children have brought these and others of their
things here to the Salvation Army thrift store, no longer able to
set a watery eye on them.

My grandmother is pulling out the most expensive things.
When she holds them up for her inspection, looking for
moth bites or broken zippers, I tell myself that I can see the
outline of the bodies of the women who once owned them
still in them. Finally, I understand, this is the poem I want
to write.

-4-

All of a sudden I am happy, finally I am thinking metaphorically.
I start to wonder; what if the life we lived, all our days, was
able to bleed into the fabric of our favorite skirt or dress. I
imagine that I can tell which clothes in my grandmother's
arms belonged to Black women and which did not. I stop
writing and watch her more carefully. Every time she lifts
something I whisper, "Yes ma'am, that one," or, "No ma'am,
not that one." Every time I say, "No," this is the one my
grandmother puts back on the rack. I am not crazy enough
to think that her secret powers and chin hairs allow her to
hear me. I am crazy enough to know we think alike about
some things. I believe that when she holds each garment up
she too can see the pain and scars, the broken dreams,
disappointments and heartaches that she knows to be the
map of too many of the lives of Black women she has known
and been.

-5-

She puts these particular dresses, the ones that Black women must have owned, back on the rack as if they were made of stained glass. She touches them with a patient tenderness I rarely see in her anymore. I think her lips are moving as she does this. I believe she is saying, *Sorry Sister Girl, I don't need no more of that in my life. Done my time with all that. The only thing I want from clothes for the rest of my life is for them to be pretty or warm.*

I look away from her and notice all the brown and white and Black people moving into the store suddenly. They are coming and going down every aisle in families and groups. I look at my watch. It is just after five o'clock. Quittin' time. Dreamin' time out in the real world. Everybody looks tired. But I notice something so clear. As they come in, in their different coming-in ways, they all seem so excited. Excited to be in the Salvation Army thrift store. Maybe they believe they are standing in a place that holds the promise of things affordable.

-6-

My grandmother startles me by walking up in my blind spot on her way over to the fifty-cent glasses. She says she needs more even though her kitchen cabinet won't completely close now because of the two hundred already there. She doesn't stop, she even crashes softly a few times into the old couches and floor lamps, saying as if they can hear, "Well, excuse me!" She turns to me before she is out of range again. "I do hope you are paying attention because everything you need to know about recycling, about what to save and what to throw away in your life, is right here." She wobbles off down the aisle giggling to herself and running over everything in her way.

Chapter Three: The Bra

-I-

My grandmother is four foot eleven and some change. Her
ninety-nine-year-old body is a small work of art to me.
Her Vaseline massaged skin is only now just starting to sag.
She has never had much for hips. Her breasts are small but
still fierce in their own way. More and more her back is
bending in like a tiny mountain giving way to that pounding
sea called old age. I am five foot eleven and a quarter with
breast enough for the whole family. Everywhere she is
small boned I am big. She is maybe a hundred pounds,
if you pour two oceans in her pocket, and I never go any-
where near bathroom scales anymore. This morning is
the last full day of her visit and this morning I could not
find my sports workout bra. The comfortable one with
no underwire, that doesn't poke me out like Miss Perfect
Body in the Victoria's Secret commercial.

-2-

I am here with her at the Salvation Army thrift store again.
This is our third straight day of shopping. We have been
here for five hours already with no lunch bell in sight. She
knows she is leaving tomorrow and so unlike all the other
days she is stopping everybody in every aisle talking to
them as if she will never see them again. She is acting as if
all weekend she has been attending some grand convention
of little old lady Salvation Army shoppers and today will
be the closing festivities. Also, she is treating the clothes
unusually bad; stepping on them and sometimes even
throwing them over the dusty splintered top of the door.
I have been following behind her like a human vacuum
cleaner. Occasionally, she wobbles up to the front counter
in between trying things on, breaking in line ahead of
others to remind the cashier that it is criminal to ask two
dollars for a wool suit that has faded from pink to peach.

-3-

The people who work here have begun to smile at me. Some even
make it a point to touch me on the shoulder when we pass
in the aisle. One even whispered yesterday, "I could never
do what you are doing." Today somebody passed by as I
sat back down at my poetry table, "I could never have the
kind of patience that you have." I smile back at them, too
polite to say what I want to say, which is, *But this is my
grandmother and I am forty-two years old and she is ninety-
nine and we are here on earth at the same time. And I am all of
who I am because she made me fried corn and cabbage every
summer day that I lived with her as a child. And every time I
entered her house as a girl there were homemade whole wheat
breadsticks and apple fritters cooling on the side of the stove.
There was blackberry juice waiting in mason jars that had
already been tendered with the natural sugary spoons of her
hands.* I want to say, *If you could still look up in the world
and still see yourself in the eyes of the one who is the very reason
you are still graciously free of madness, then you would do
whatever you had to do for her. Wouldn't you?*

But all that's private so I go back to looking down the rows.
Somebody I don't know sees me searching and points to
the dressing room area as if they know who I must be look-
ing for. I just smile and thank her with a nod of my head.

-4-

There are only two tiny dressing rooms. There are people wait-
ing in a line to use them both. There are lots of people waiting
in line. My grandmother has made one of the rooms her home
away from home. Her movements are pretty slow. It takes her
a long time to pull each dress down around her. My job is to
return anything she does not want to the racks. She does not
allow me to help her dress or undress. I reach to tap on the
left side door because walking towards it I notice a hundred
dresses already on the floor. I can hear my grandmother

shouting through the door at the line of people telling them to be nice, "In Jesus name be nice!" She even counsels them through the door that they might consider leaving and trying the other Salvation Army thrift store on the west side of town if they are in such a hurry. I have no idea how she knows about the other store. I smile and back away from the line of people standing before the dressing room doors. I pray that they have grandmothers at home.

-5-

I pop my head inside the dressing room door. She is there with a jungle of tops and bottoms and a sea of chiffon all around her feet. Just as I am about to take an armload of clothes back outside past the mob of waiters, I look at her and there is my lost sports bra. It is double wrapped around her small upper body like a body bandage. It is twisted and looped all around her like a bad seat belt that has been in several accidents. Somehow it is holding everything on her in; womanly, tight, and youthful. I start laughing and the clothes start falling and she starts swatting me with a blue seersucker jumper. "Something must be mighty funny for you to keep that door open so long for to give me The Pneumonia."

I stop laughing long enough to point to her upper body and she finally looks down around at herself. She pokes up real close to the looking glass, straightens out her trifocals, leaning even closer to the mirror. It all comes into focus for her. "Lord Baby, that's why everything fittin' me so good today." We are laughing harder than we have ever laughed before.

-6-

As we exit the store the clerks are still shaking their heads. The manager passes by saying, "I have never seen two like you before." I know he has never seen two like us before. Because there has never been one like her before.

One tall. One short. One fifty-seven years older than the other. The little girls inside us both still so pristinely intact and falling more and more in love with each other even as we grow older by the day and our bodies prepare for recycling, to say their good-byes, but not our hearts, never our hearts.

Chapter Four: The Cancer

-1-

I am my grandmother's oldest granddaughter. Right from the start we knew we belonged to each other. On October 16th in the last year of all those 9s and six months, long after we left our twin mark on the Southside Salvation Army thrift store in Kentucky, I drove all day to be with her in the land of our birth, South Carolina. For several weeks I had been driving home every weekend, we didn't know when or how or if. The doctor said "three months" but Ma Bea said *only God could know that.* When I walked in the door Mama said, *She's been waiting for you and only you.* I walked over to the bed. She looked at me then turned away disgusted at not being able to reach for me or command her physical body with the same precision that she had for ninety-nine years. She could no longer speak but I knew she knew I was there.

-2-

For some reason her feet wouldn't stay under the cover of her bed. For two hours I held her right foot in my left hand and her left foot in my right, warming them with my body. Her little legs were still powerful and pumping so hard. Once she almost pushed me back against the wall. She seemed to be trying to run away. That's when Mama said what almost broke my water, "Look at us, three generations of woman."

I raised my eyes to the ceiling and pushed the rising salt back down. Ma Bea was staring at me, still hard and hopeful. Mama said the nurse had just left. She had put a brand-new pain patch on her arm and whispered that Ma Bea's esophagus was now no bigger than a straw. I listened to her raspy rattling breath, watched her labor for every inhale. She stared at me like she was waiting for me to help her as I always had. I kept kissing her hands, humming back the salt, rubbing her feet and talking to her. Out of Ma Bea's direct sight Mama started to shake.

-3-

In May when we received the diagnosis we had decided as a family to take care of Ma Bea in her own home. I had moved in and lived with her over the summer and then Mama came and stayed while I went back to teaching. As the cancer took more and more of her body away Mama waited on Ma Bea with a brilliant seamless devotion.

-4-

They say that a daughter comes through the belly of her mother but through the spirit of her grandmother. Standing there before them both I realized this was the roundest moment of my life. I had no children. But my mother had become my grandmother's mother and I had become mother and daughter to them both. All our female lines and edges had fallen into each other. I stared at Mama. The only daughter who had given birth to an only daughter. Her soft brown face was starting to show the wear and tear of both loss and birth. I knew better than to look at any mirror.

-5-

A new kind of recognition was settling in now. Mama began whispering two things back and forth to all of us standing there in the room. "I've never seen her do this before," she said nervously. "Do you think this is it?" My hands kept going from my grandmother to my mother, who sometimes fell on her knees beside the bed in prayer when she got no earthly answers to her questions. Ma Bea's legs were still full of great motion. Arms and feet moving strong and fast. She was unable to control them but she was still so willful. She was so determined to not go, even on this last journey, without a fight. She wanted to tell us something but nothing was able to exit her mouth anymore. I kept reassuring her that I could hear her and in a way I could. My hands bloomed into desperate ears cupped tight around her feet. I could hear her trying to run, could feel her tapping out final instructions.

-6-

At 8:50 Ma Bea stopped blinking. At 8:57 she took a breath so deep it seemed to stop the clock that Mama was staring at. Her beautiful pretty ankles went quiet in my hands and she finally stopped trying to run. My salt blocks cracked wide and family soon slowly encircled the bed.

-7-

After wide hugs and great tears I searched the dresser tops and drawers in my grandmother's bedroom but found none. I finally asked my uncle if he had any pennies on him. He reached into his pocket and pulled out two brand-new 1999 copper suns. After Daddy said the prayer and Brother No. 1 crossed her arms across her chest I kissed the pennies then closed down the eyes of the woman who had taught me how to see.

-8-

The funeral home came at midnight. My father and my brothers carried Ma Bea out of her old home house and into the back of the loneliest car in the world. Daddy said it was tradition. He said, *We carry our own as far as we can.* As they passed by us in the yard my hands reached to touch the corners of the ocean-blue velvet coverlet that draped her.

After the car pulled off I was unable to sleep. I stood there on the porch for hours. In my mind I kept seeing the long car moving down the small dark street away from all of us. The wind started to pick up stronger by the minute. At two that morning the winds of Hurricane Irene hit South Carolina. I was still standing on the porch when everything started to bend down low. I hadn't heard the news about Irene coming. I had been busy tending to the last breaths of another hurricane. In that good-bye moment everything seemed related, connected, and nothing out of the ordinary.

-9-

I was my grandmother's heart. We belonged to each other. She had taught me to believe in things unseen. Even before the long car was out of sight I was rubbing my chin and waiting for a sign from her that she was alright. Standing there in the middle of her ocean of brilliant pansies and begonias, I watched old pine and oak sway like summoned dancers then bend forward like servants. And just before the birth of her favorite time of day, with a soft suddenness, I felt the warm heavy wind of the Great Mother lift the plain dutiful life of another great mother to the wild beyond.

I wish I could put my arms around my people and fly away.

—IDA B. WELLS-BARNETT

The Greatest Show on Earth

for Saartjie Baartman, Joice Heth, Anarcha of Alabama, Truginini, and us all.

Under glass and tent
floating in formaldehyde jelly
curled in a deadman's float
live the split spread
unanesthetized legs
of Black women
broken like the stirrups
of a wishbone,

somebody got their wish
and somebody didn't.

The lilac plumage
of our petalled genitalia,
in all its royal mauve
and plum rose,
with matching eggplant hips
that pull the ocean
across itself each night,
boats of peanut skin
folded and rolled
like the new fur,
all proof of our pathology
all cut away
by pornographic hands
fascinated with difference
and the spectacle
of being a Black woman,

so the normal pay their fifty cents
to see what makes a freak a freak.

     Go ahead,
     walk around her
     she won't bite,
     she is the headless woman,
     see her protruding mass,
     steatopygia.

We don't have to be dead first
to be cut into manageable size,
one that fits their measuring rods,
their medicine chests will not rest
until we are properly pried,
it has always been about
opening us up,
experimenting with Black women
but never dissecting their own desires.

The sideshow
was pitched on our backs,
the speculum hammered out
between our legs,
modern medicine founded
on the world of our hips;
we the standard patterned girth
of every bustle skirt ever made.

Black woman as spectacle,
wanting to but afraid to die.
Knowing death would never end
such sterling silver lust.
Bodies quake whole lifetimes
in a national geographic tremble
until the obituary arrives:

Bury me behind the mountains,
so they can never find me again.

But they do find us,
do dig us back up,
retrieve the last swatches
of soft skin,
the last twig of curved brown bone.

Our opened pirouetting vaginas,
our African music boxes
whittled down to perfect
change-purse size,

for the normal
who will always pay
their fifty cents
to be sure and see
what makes a freak
a freak.

SHARK BITE

Some things should never be eaten
or held anywhere near the mouth,
even when served in the best restaurant.

A germ of history
four hundred years old
can enter the meat,

even when exquisitely seasoned,
perfectly cooked, the chef award-winning,
the cutting board bleached daily.

In celebration of something forgotten now
I ordered shark for the first time,
and my belly remembered what I had not.

Cannibal suddenly to my own history;
one dark, beautiful, devoured human being
going down my pipes like a chunk of lye,

lye made to straighten hair, not intestines.
Her scream hit the bottom of my belly lining,
her legs stretched out behind her

as if ninety days in the gut
of a slaver's ship was long enough,

to be bent in a circle like a closed padlock,
suddenly in me she needed room
to stay alive.

She kicked with her long Black woman foot
and my fingers released the linen napkin
in my lap. I touched for the hole in my middle,

and the delicious fish, the tender shark,
bloomed into a memory nova that
I did not know was there, and there

was the story of a woman being raped
by nineteen men in shiny pilgrim shoes,

and the wondrous shark became
all 999 muscles of one brown man,
resisting his forced daily feeding again,

the whiskered fish was in the net of the schooner,
pulling down heavy in the middle, as an obedient
brown bean of a child was told one last time to

fly.

Later that night as I stooped over
trying one final time to bring it all up,
through a curtain chill of tears,

every delicious miserable bite
sixty million and more
hands wringing my stomach,

like dirty wash that wouldn't come clean.
I wrestled with sheets and pillowcases
and memory to find quiet, peace.

There was a ship,
the *Henrietta Marie,*
breaking against the furious water,

and there were shackles
and the woman on deck
her legs open in the hiss of a scream,

and the man refusing to eat or live
reaching for her
and the child finally flying,

and I was there too,
unfurling with them all,

pushing my legs back
out of their comfortable
ladylike curl,
like a shark smelling water
in her blood.

SIGN LANGUAGE

for the man who jumped out in front of the woman with his arm raised like a machete screaming Abomination! as she walked the streets of San Francisco holding her lover's hand for the first time in public

There is a woman who goes to sleep
every night wishing she had broken
your sternum reached up inside your
chest momentarily borrowing your
heart to hold before your screaming
face and with her other hand still
clutching her lover's broke next into
her own sternum plucking next her
own heart dangling them both there
sterling silver sign language for you
tell me what is the difference.

The New Cotton

They are just boys, chain
ganged to the side of the road,
dressed to the 9s in sunny
orange, that shade of red that
never seems to set, familiar
color of some foreign flower,
the kind you can close your
eyes in sleep and still see, but
these boys are not flowers
anymore, no
thing that can be seen to bloom
has been left to bloom, in this
place where a chain around a
Black man's ankle is the state
jewel, but if you still own your
eyes you know they are still
just boys.
They do not yet know how to
bend, someone has not yet
passed on the secret
of how to save their backs
for the rest of the journey,
someone forgot to offer the old
old way of how to get through
the whip of their young days
in order to reach the sweet
rock of their old, they angle
and arc carelessly,
not knowing they are match-
sticks of American history,

never squatting down low
in the grass, never bending
at the ankle or thigh, they are
such proud brittle lion trees
about to break in every
direction, but free, the weave
of all their fabric wasted in the
constant picking up of useless
plastic side-of-the-road things,
that as I get closer,
that as I pass,
look white and sticky plump,
some kind of new cotton
stuck inside their reaching
Robeson hands.

THE GIRLFRIEND'S TRAIN

You write like a Black woman who's never been hit before.

I read poetry in Philly
for the first time ever.
She started walking up,
all the way, from in back
of the room.

From against the wall
she came,
big coat, boots,
eyes soft as candles
in two storms blowing.

Something she could not see
from way back there but
could clearly hear in my voice,
something she needed to know
before pouring herself back out
into the icy city night.

She came close to get a good look,
to ask me something she found
in a strange way missing
from my Black woman poetry.

Sidestepping the crowd
ignoring the book signing line,
she stood there waiting
for everyone to go, waiting
like some kind of Representative.

And when it was just the two of us
she stepped into the shoes of her words:
Hey,

>*You write real soft.*
>*Spell it out kind.*
>*No bullet holes,*
>*No open wounds,*
>*In your words.*
>*How you do that?*
>*Write like you never been hit before?*

I could hardly speak,
all my breath held ransom
by her question.

I looked at her and thought, maybe,
there was a train on pause somewhere,
maybe just outside the back door
where she had stood, listening.

A train with boxcars
that she was escorting somewhere,
when she heard about the reading
and came in.

A train with boxcars
carrying broken women's bodies,
their carved-up legs and bullet-riddled
stomachs momentarily on pause
from moving cross-country.

Women's bodies;
brown, black-and-blue,
lying right where coal, cars,
and cattle usually do.

She needed my answer
for herself and for them too.
Hey,

> *We were just wondering*
> *how you made it through*
> *and we didn't?*

I shook my head.
I had never thought about
having never been hit
and what it might have
made me sound like.

> *Guess how many times I been stabbed?*

She raised her blouse
all the way above her breasts,
the cuts on her resembling
some kind of grotesque wallpaper.

How many women are there like you?

Then I knew for sure.

She had been sent in from the Philly cold,
by the others on the train,
to listen, stand up close,
to make me out as best she could.

She put my hand overtop hers,
asked could we stand up
straight back to straight back,
measure out our differences
right then and there.

She gathered it all up,
wrote down the things she could,
remembering the rest to the trainload
of us waiting out back for answers.

Full to the brim with every age
of woman, every neighborhood
of woman, whose name
had already been forgotten.

The train blew its whistle,
she started to hurry.

I moved towards her
and we stood back-to-back,
her hand grazing the top
of our heads,
my hand measuring out
our same widths,
each of us recognizing
the brown woman latitudes,
the Black woman longitudes
in the other.

I turned around,
held up my shirt,
and brought my smooth belly
into her scarred one;
our navels pressing,
marking out some kind of new
equatorial line.

HATE

Arthur Ravenel, Republican Senator from South Carolina, called the NAACP the "National Association for Retarded People" at a Confederate flag support rally. He later said, "I made a mistake and I feel very badly about it because I said retarded people and I have a retarded son." He also added, "That does not mean I'm apologizing to the NAACP."

—*JET*, JANUARY 31, 2000

How does a father
with a son struggling
to be seen whole
in the eyes of the world
forget the son long enough
for a slip of the tongue
to be recorded forever
for posterity's sake?

How does a father not think
that a son will ever know
what he said that day at the rally
when he slipped
and he, the father, revealed
his true feelings
about him, the son,
the same feelings he feels
about other different people?

How does a father
slip off one tongue
while he is rallying
his Confederate troops
and slip on another
later

after the rally
when he is home
with his son,
gentle inheritor of his name?

He does not.
The slippery tongue
is one and the same.

What could make you
forget your son?
A fight over an old flag?
The heat from a simmering
hundred-year-old war?

Hate stops at nothing.
Not even the sacred door
of a son's private room.

EASY-BAKE

Go home and tell your daughters they are beautiful.

—STOKELY CARMICHAEL

Every day there are more sightings,
children latched to guns are in this year.
School shootings all the rage.

Especially young girls who don't want
to be girlfriends anymore. They, the widest
target, the largest pile of bodies.

White boys with high-powered rifles shirk,
take position behind flowering trees, the birthday
bow still tied in a knot at the trigger, their sights
set on the whole school yard, the whole prayer
circle.

In the crosshairs, flipping back and forth,
is it a deer grazing peacefully, or a little girl
saying *No.*

Across town, Black boys prefer close range,
hot pistols no bigger than their hands burn
their six-pack stomachs, they call out another
Black boy's name, *On your mark, get set,*
Bitch.

In the news this morning, right beside
the most recent school shooting, advertisements;
toy Easy-Bake ovens with the caption,
"What Every Little Girl Wants!"

My eyes zoom in back and forth.
The bodies of the girls are rolled out
covered in white sheets, a mother is
screaming her way through the crowd.

Inside the doors of those Easy-Bake ovens
I imagine a place for bulletproof shields,
something for the unspoken, for after
we teach our daughters to cook, clean, and
walk two steps behind any man;
as long as he is that.

I imagine a matching ensemble, an Easy-Bake
vest and shield, so that they might defend themselves
from what we are teaching our sons.

LABOR STRIKE

Black girl
bobbin' on the Wednesday street,
McDonald's pencil
layin' back
'cross her ear,
like she ain't at work
and heretofore
from now on
for evermore
is refusin' to take
your orders.

MY OLD KENTUCKY HOME
Where the Darkies Are Gay*

From the week of October 25, 1994, after the killing of eighteen-year-old Antonio Sullivan, shot in the head at close range by a policeman.

What I See: Shiloh Baptist Church

At the funeral, young Black men glide in,
still in school clothes. They file into the old
neighborhood church looking around like
strangers. Their books, folded and silent, sit
back behind them on wooden pews like the
bricks of a hundred frozen futures.

A steady stream of boy-men wet down
every aisle. They lean into the netted open
arms of each other. I notice, on them nothing
fits, their pants, their shirts, their fear,
everything is too big.

A domino of young men from every local
village, eyes bursting like tall hydrants, they
circle around his open casket, brown faces
shining, spotlights pointed, beating, lasered
toward him like the last resort of some kind
of power source.

They huddle, afraid of the death staring up
at them, but they are more terrified of leaving
him there, alone, so they break the rules. They

*Original lyrics of the state song of Kentucky

linger and the service cannot start, not until
they leave him and sit down. But they hover
like a hundred humps in a gigantic umbrella,
they, his last protection. We see the downpour
begin. They stand so long by his side, their
ocean of eyes begging,
Wake up!

They lean on his chrome baby-blue capsule.
They have their private conversations. One
of them, as if he has seen it done in a movie,
runs his long brown fingers in front of his
eyes like windshield wipers just to make sure.
A hundred lampposts all curving in to see
what their eyes cannot believe.

They make for him a silvery black moon
of themselves. They crescent a way into his
last earth memory. They greet him for the last
time in their tradition, by tucking things down
and under his cardboard body for his final journey.

They put private male things all around him.
Things we can't see from our seats. It is an old
Affrilachian mountain custom, to put things
in the pocket of the young dead, it is done
in grand hip-hop style.

I want them to take off their hats in God's house.
This is what I want, what my mother and father
and grandparents would want. What others who
think they know what it is like to be Black and
young and male, raised on the east side of this
top-one-hundred mid-American city, want,
but this is not what they do.

These invisible sons of invisible sons, these
grieving corn-rowed young eagles do not
remove their hats. They do turn the brims
of them around from front to back. They have
their way and you have yours. Finally they
leave him there and scatter out into the pews,
by twos and threes and tens, walking. Stumbling
into the stark white light of TV cameras. They
are so blinded by how he did not get up this time,
not this time.

The organ music takes over now. They walk
out like crippled men, so much older and slower
than before. These veterans of community world
wars, numbers three and four, lift their heads.
Anyone with half a heart can see the birthmarks
of greasepaint smeared across cheeks and chests.
They walk away, readying themselves for a life
of more war, more battle.

Life will not wait for them to finish their mourning.
It will call them back to the land of the living-dead
before they are ready. By the nape of their mother-
given necks: Jerome, Earl, Robert, Willie Lucius,
Willie James Junior, will return to the front lines
alongside the ghosts of their fight-the-good-fight
fathers.

What I Dream: The Lexington Cemetery

When they run out of burial land (and they will
at the rate we are going) the already-dead will
be the ones who will save us. Those who have
been gone for a hundred years or more will be

the ones who will finally give us the life we don't
seem to know how to create together.

Every set of bones over one hundred will be
moved to one mass grave site, set aside by the
Commonwealth. It will be commandment: all
must leave their private single dwellings and
be made to mix-mingle with others unlike
themselves.

It will be law, passed by House, Senate
committee, Frankfort lobbyist, even crooked
good-old-boy Kentucky politicians. They will
think they are saving precious, irreplaceable
Bluegrass farms, but they will be saving more.

Henry Clay, statesman and winningest politician,
will lie beside Isaac Murphy, statesman and
winningest jockey, and when the dust has settled
on that new day he will ask what he always
wanted to know, *What was it like to ride an
animal so fast?* And Murphy will answer,
Like signing the wind into law.

Those dead a hundred years or more will just
be deemed "the expendable dead." They won't
be the Black dead or the white dead, the rich dead,
the poor dead, or the revered. They will just be the
dead. We will have to do this because we will no
longer have the space to be as thoughtful about the dead,
because we have been so thoughtless about the living.

And so the salt trucks will move through the award-
winning Lexington cemetery gathering up the bones
of all centenarians. The same trucks will cross the
train tracks and amble through the sacred overgrown

African graveyard no. 2, gathering up everyone certified
over one hundred years. All will be moved to the prepared
mass grave that was once an old horse farm. This
will be the new law of the old land.

There won't be room to convene about it. Money won't
matter. Family stock won't change any minds. It won't
be a question of race or baptism, pedigree, class or
Did your family buy or were they sold on Cheapside Street?

Black and white finally skinless and naked to the bone
will be taken away to live together. The seventy- and eighty-
year-old youngsters left standing on the corner will say
out loud as the rattling salt trucks pull away, *Well I
never thought I would live to see the dead give us this day
our daily bread.*

And finally, there in the common denominator
of their hundred years of death, and by the common
denominator of the survival of the living, the fear
will be no more. Finally, white bones will fall and
snuggle up next to black bones, and no one will care
or be able to tell who was ever who.

And the talking, save the hugging, that needed to
happen last week, light-years before he shot him
and he fell dead and everybody who knew him
took to the streets hurting like hunger, while
everybody else hurled *Riot!* out into the autumn
wind like an aperitif. The talking will finally happen.

Cheekbone to cheekbone up close, black femurs will
touch white metacarpals and white eye sockets will
soften back at black eye sockets noticing that they once
were blessed with sight but chose not to see. Black
shins will graze white shins, white funny bones will

even crook around black funny bones and laughter
will roll in like a late evening train. Because the only thing
left will be bones. No memory to pass, no skin to fear.

Dead folks long gone, without a memory to keep
hate alive, without a mind to remind them of a
racist word or deed, without a family trait, tradition,
stereotype, hurtful dismissing glance, without skin
to designate the racial tribe, will be left to create on
this earth what we were supposed to create all along.

What I Think: The Press Conference

The year will be 2595. The archaeologist will read
from his detailed report. He will be an incredibly
well-known theorist with a brilliant scientific mind,
exact in his capacity to explain what life on earth
was like in 1994, six hundred and seventy-one years before.

Just how did people live together on this land? This
will be the hot topic of the day. He will stand
before the floating computer monitor and report
that even though it has been a two-billion-dollar,
fifty-year study, there are still some unanswered
questions: like how the darker ones of the species
(not all but certainly far too many for it to have been
mere coincidence), and primarily the young adult
males, all had these strange holes searing some part
of their craniums.

He will say his research shows that the holes were
put there by some type of hunting invention and
*We are still exploring how this condition could have
been so prevalent.* He will add that just because

there is no reasonable explanation does not mean
there is no explanation at all. He assures more money
will help uncover the answer.

He will recall several times during the report
that the society back then as a whole was highly
technologically advanced. He will say that it does
not really make sense. He will look perplexed, take
off his glasses, and eventually put his notes away.
As the news conference ends he will conclude his
findings:

It is all very strange to us. As strange as the last
finding, which we had not seen evidence of since
A.D. 79 a continent away, in the city of Pompeii,
the mummified bodies of the smaller children
in the same Kentucky project houses, found crouching
in corners, ninety-nine percent of whom seemed
to have died with their mouths wide open,
as if in the middle of one long unbroken scream.

It's not that complicated, but you're gonna need a bulletproof soul.

—SADE, *LOVERS ROCK*

AFRO-GREGORIAN CHANT

The wild monks sing
and my fingers are pushed for good,

eight hours wafered,
the perfect food for the broiled toast

of your sleeping knees.
The Great Smoky Mountains

fall in on us,
Cherokee trees curl liquid smoke

and I am alone with the curve
of the road and a missing hand,

which now has fallen asleep beneath,
along with the rest of you.

This is the holiest of life.
The castanetting call of celibate men

frolicking the air,
Gregorian monks chant away spanishly,

as the shawl of Appalachia is thrown,
and you asleep through it all,

missing the bloom of God in fall
and the salt of palmetto shores closing in.

As the sun bakes your face
through the tempered stained glass

into the holiday warm of pecan pie,
the soft mouths of chosen chanters

turn to wedding bells;
while inside the pine

and the baobab
the everywhere eyes

of mere lovers
boil.

FROGLEGS

In bed at night
the bottom half of her
never sleeps.

Her legs,
ocean tendril
of mad motion
even when the rest
of her
decides to call it
a day.

All day long
she has moved
through the world
a Black woman,
at night
she sleeps
like one too.

Restless
on land,
restless
at sea.

Her beautiful
bouquet of legs
disregarding the rest
of her higher education;

running her
in place,
spinning her
amphibiously
around.

Sex

After "Oh, what would you know about it anyway?"

How the room rained down
a mother's only blistering ash,
her words lifting then settling
clear and hot, then the branding
of me complete.

After she proclaimed,
to the rest of the family,
that whatever it is that I do
with another woman
could never even-steven
to what she does with Daddy.

As if my way to human pleasure was
too inefficient to be called the same.
As if we who do with a woman
should find a new name for the doing.

She believing that my body
coming together with another
woman's, a fake freak of nature,
not sex or love and could never be.

The sermon of her looks
always the same.

How my pot of woman
is not worth its salt,
because there is not the pepper
of a man there.

That in order for any woman
to cook up a thing worth
sensually serving,
a lid and seasoning
of a certain fit and taste
are required.

That what I offer to the diamond
and life of another woman, that
then streams up my two front
female spines, that branches off
into a desert orchid, that grows
into a family of complicated
spiraled things in the middle
of any hot springs geyser night,
is not worth its weight in sweat.

As if what I know about pleasure
and the microscopic fittings of love,
about the filling of an appetite
that lives somewhere between
cerebellum and thigh tissue,
that runs like a southern railroad
trestle to my heart bone emptying
next into my lung sacs, as if that
tenderness which douses all the gates
of my body clean and wet like all
the steamed water and wind that
ever were in the world, suddenly
let loose, as if what comes from
the zest and tongue of another
woman's capsule to my own,
that intricate complicated vessel
of how and what we shape our

loving into cannot be compared
to what she has felt between her
own gulf stream.

Mama, what appears shut sky
to you is heaven opened wide
to me.

THE DIVE

(The Turtle Suite Poems)

So there's nothing left—
What can I say other than take care of yourself?

—CURTIS MAYFIELD

The weight of the world is less underwater
As you leave I submerge   Begin the moving
through   With everything unfinished between
us   Hoisted high upon my back   Tied down like
winter tinder   This the deep freeze dive   My
green-brown shell heavy   All the way to the oval
edge   With all I believed would always be   The
salt water helps   Lifting all of it from me without
taking anything away   The sweet scorched things
still try to flee   Like a school of red bandana fish
The Geechee blue wedding roof blown off in the storm
Rice and popcorn piled high   Scattered out of their
smoldering bowls   Along with the most singed
memory of them all   Your curtain of brown eyes
opens   First thing in the blackberry morning
Sweet things bobble and put up a good fight
Refuse to fall   All treasures from a shipwreck
Now piled high
Submerged now
Underwater now
The nest destroyed
The sharpest hook
Ruthless fire pirate
Love

STEAMED RICE

(The Turtle Suite Poems)

In me nothing is extinguished or forgotten.
—PABLO NERUDA

When we were married,
we always ate one bowl
of steamed rice first,
ritual appetizer
you said,
to clean
prepare
the mouth
for the rest of the meal
on the way.

      Soon come
      pungent garlic,
      lilting Scotch bonnet,
      circling behind us
      on the stove
      in a curtain of curling heat.

Now that we are not,
I long for one bowl
of rice reversed,
with steam enough
to pull your carpet
of chocolate pepper
from the roof
of my mouth.

Where does a black soul go to rest?

—RANDALL ROBINSON

METALLURGY

for Cassandra Wilson

She's the one who won't leave us.

She sings and cobwebs are strung
like salve, like liniment laced,
every note forging iron.

Her low sulfur notes swim
in a buttered brine. Her reddened mouth
parachutes around leaping Africans,
resuscitating the butter-bean breath of Black boys.

She keeps bringing up the past
like it's a throat,
with a muddy Mississippi fish bone
stuck crossways.

At her Marian Anderson table we always eat our fill.

She opens like a furnace (all southern),
walks us to the flame (all polite),
refuses to enter the pretty waters of the melody
without the rest of the scorched story in tow.

She sees to the keeping of the shells,
studies the motions of Black mermaids
draped in crepe myrtle,
waist high in red-dirt octaves.
She learns it back to us
by way of the highway of the ear.

Before the end of the song
we check our wrists,
we lick our lips,
we taste ankle iron.

She's the one who won't abandon.

On stage, under lights, she's slipping
through the thicket again, untying
Grandmama's hands, every gnarled
throat in the room straightens, finally
free of scuppernong, wisteria.

She enters the room
and a valley of blackbirds takes off,
the furnace opens and closes,
all the copper in us turns toward
the magnet of her breath.
Every penny we've ever saved
in mason jars, for the ritual closing
of the eyes, rattles.

Her coral-indigo humming raises
adolescent cousins full-term, pouring
salt into the historical wound. When
her eyes close on the clef of treble,
when her head goes back past the
beginning of hypnosis, she is seeing
things again.

The Atlantic Ocean's greatest slaughter
is scribbled beneath her lids in
scarred black codes.

With or without guitar she can pluck you.

She enters counterclockwise
all the while in ring shout time
Slipping slew-footed mildly like a monk,
round and round the floor
until gold is discovered
in the pan of her feet.
In half notes she flutters.

She's the one who won't leave us.

A girl from Jackson, from where daughters
in concert are raised only once, given African guitars,
then taught the iron songs, instead of
bedtime stories, then set upon the world.

Songs that tell
how never to leave,
how never to leave us,
how never to leave well enough alone.

Assam

Old Black woman heavyweight,
body conscious now,
after years of swinging
wide chocolate wings
below her waist,
wedged now into the surf for good,
her treasures
sunk into the sand
of self-consciousness.

From her throne
she watches more than moves
these days.
I walk by noticing;
things still pull to her,
the uncalled water
knocks softly,
bubbling about
her flat-out thighs,
the wet salt wanting in,
no matter.

Her fingers disobey
the rest of her
and climb down.
Alone, they turn
into years
of summer grandchildren
running from the chasing water
straight into her netted arms.

She sits,
dripping
half in half out
the sea,
a tea bag full
of black uncut leaves,
without you, I whisper,
the world is plain
tap water.

"A Hero Ain't Nothin' but a Sandwich"

—ALICE CHILDRESS

In Atlanta two men and a high-rise building on fire.
The one building it, who set it aflame, with his good
hands, still on top pushed into its last heavenly corner.

The other flying around, dangling from a rope
dropped from a helicopter, his good hands
desperately trying to reach.

One Black man, one white.

A tiny opening of air and the helicopter slips
through the smoke. They peel out their open arms
to each other.

One of them wraps his legs about the other.
It is a fireman's way of rescue.
In a loverly embrace they face each other
all the way back down to earth.

Once back on ground they are safe.
Life gets back to normal. But I'm not ready
for them to be safe and life as normal hasn't
worked in four hundred years.

I want them to zoom the helicopter back up.
I want them to lock their legs back tight around each other.
I want the sight of them clasped there like a statement
to answer something more than an accident.

Their bodies dancing down, their gallant
purple hearts staring, iris to slow-dragging iris.
Make the beautiful sight of that
linger longer than highlights on the nightly news.

Not one more feel-good story about one more
local hero, patted on the back, only to be
forgotten, only because he was only doing what he
was only trained to do, nothing more, nothing else.

But before they zoom back up, recategorize it.

Call out what keeps us from each other's daily arms
what it is. Call hatred by its first name; a firestorm,
category 1; the kind that burns whole countries down.

And whosoever is flying the helicopter
with all of us in it,
apologize for the inconvenience
but go ahead and announce
that none of us can come down
until every flame is out.

THE MAKING OF PAPER

for Toni Cade Bambara, 1939–1995

In the early 1980s I spent two years in a writing workshop that the writer Toni Cade Bambara held in her house in Atlanta every first Sunday. Anybody in the community who was writing was welcome: students, bus drivers, carpenters. I adored the opportunity to sit at this great writer's feet. She knew so much about so much. She later moved to Philadelphia. She was later diagnosed with cancer. We talked on the long-distance line when we could. I would always ask was there anything she needed that I could send. She usually answered no. But in our last conversation, which took place one week before she crossed over, she held the phone a little longer. "Maybe . . ." she said, ". . . maybe you could send some paper, and what about one of those fat juicy pens?"

Imagine that,
you asking me for paper.

For the record let me state:
I would hunt a tree down for you,
stalk it until it fell
all loud and out of breath
in the forest.
Much as I love a tree;
fat, tall, and free.
As antiviolent and provegetarian
as I am.

Never much
for strapping a gun
to any of my many hips,
for any reason whatsoever,
but on the copper penny eyes
of my grandmother, I tell you
this: I would hunt a tree down for you.

And when found
I would pull it all the way down the road
through congested city streets all by myself
and deliver it straightaway
to your hospital bed,
one single extra-large floral arrangement,
something loud and free,
with red and purple bow.

Or better yet,
this tree-loving
gun-hating Geechee girl
would strap a Wild West
gun belt–machete
around her hips
enter the worst part of the woods alone
and go trunk to trunk
until the right one appeared
growing peaceful in its thousand-year-old
natal pot.

Look it
right in its
round rough ancient eyes
and confess away,
tell it straight to its woody face,
my about-to-do deed.

I'd even touch it
on its limbs,
fingers begging forgiveness,
give as much comfort to it
as I could, while trying to
explain the necessaryness
of its impending death;
me standing there,

My *Gorilla, My Love* eyes
spilling all over everything,
sending up papyrus prayers
that all begin with,
"I'm so sorry but Toni Cade needs paper."

Only then would I slash its lovely body
into one million thin black cotton rag sheets,
just your uncompromising size.

Send you some paper?
Oh yes,
paper is coming Toni Cade
wagonloads
in the name
of your sweet Black writing life,
from Black writers everywhere
refusing to leave
the arena
to the fools.

Paper is on the way.

FISHING AMONG THE LEARNED

i

On the banks of her butterfly pond
Grandmother would stand,
as fluid as a waterfall, teaching
with a five-and-dime pole in her hand,
Be still and listen to that,
she could be heard to say.

She would make more good decisions,
lose more control, gain, relinquish power,
care about more people, recycle energy,
discern more foolishness
in an afternoon of fishing
than Congress ever could
be they all Democrat, all Republican.

My first semesters ever were spent
staring up at this Human University,
shifting my weight from bamboo leg
to trout flat foot, waving first cow fly
then firefly from off her apron dress,
listening to the sounds swelling
around us, there was noise, there
was instruction, there was a difference
in the two.

This kind of standing stare at still water;
Fresh Water Philosophy, this speaking on
the depths of a true life lived full; Saturday

Sociology, footprints baked into the soft
bank; Advanced Lucy Geography. These
outdoor lessons could go on for days and
did, as long as there was sun and bait there
was learning.

To educate means to lead out,
she whispered to me on the snakish road
home. I had no idea what she was saying
or why now.

At well-lit nightfall in between the quiver
of country bugs I'd wonder why she'd stood
me there, that pole in my hand gripped tight
as teeth full born to a jaw insisting, *Girl,*
pond water is as good as any book.

She'd already said to me in dreams, *A good*
teacher can do more than talk about it, she
can see it beyond the convincing skinny pages
of any flattened tree.

There on that bank preparing me for giant
whales when she knew full well bream and
mullet were all we had tugging our lines.

You don't fish just to catch, you fish so you
can keep, so you can put something back,
the fisherwoman taught. *It has less to do*
with the fish and more to do with your line
staying in the water, with your hand on the
pole, with discerning rituals, sniffing out the
weather, with what you can figure out about
yourself that early in the quiet morning in
between the iridescent help of sun or moon,
in between the magnificent bites.

Know what you will not let corrupt you, that
you cannot be bought or sold, assume another
will come after you have gone, their own pole
tight in hand as well hoping to catch something.
Put something back whenever you can. Then she'd
untie the hook from its mouth, lay it back
in the soft velvet water, her fingers already
asking forgiveness.

Now that is something to keep.

ii

I cast out among the learned and teach
to alter sleeping states. I stand before the
university pond and fish for the living who
send air bubbles up to the learned who know
real life bestows no terminal degrees.

I have come to know that we all dangle here,
grub and silkworms alike casting out our
many different lines. The well baited and the
barely hooked while the new recruits watch,
the old sentries look out silently. We push away
from shore annually, calling our rolls like salmon,
pole-vaulting, determined to remember the old
ways to wisdom, do or die.

Fishing is the key to everything that moves.

A poet needs to fly-fish in the middle of the
bluest grass in order to catch glimpses of
the privileged information; that there are too
many meetings and not enough conversations
going on. A poet needs to stand girded before the

listening eyes of those who pay their hard-earned
money wondering, *Will I teach them anything that
the world will later ask of them to be sure and know?*

I must.

Inside the polished granite of academe
a poet must hope beyond hope that we will
all keep fishing at the bank and one day forgo
the carnivorous weigh-in, the comparison of
scales, and instead throw our prime catch back
while keeping the feeling of casting out close.

A poet invited to the marble table must cast out
a cat gut cord, a thousand-pound live wire,
with hook enough for all and reel in everything
she sees and speak of the good with the bad
and hope for the best, do or die.

And cocoon along with the rest spinning for
silk, for sheepskin, for sanity, for something
higher, more enduring than sweet tenure
or paper trails, for the high and honored art
of teaching, of returning something real to the
mental food chain; to transform one single life.

I stand I cast I feel I fish for something
that lives here in these waters, something
some of us have hooked but most have never
pulled all the way to the surface, something
we'll eternally feel nibbling on our lines but
never lay our eyes free and flat upon if we do
not study the scholarship of fishing.

In the spirit of the old blind ones, those who
would take their chances in a heartbeat, pull
up safe anchor, all their eggs trembling in one
basket, throw your line out a little farther
tomorrow. Remember their commandment:
"If you do what you've always done,
you're gonna get what you've always got."

Don't pull your line in too fast,
Grandmother would say out of the corner of her eye,
Keep your hook in the water all the way to the edge,
that's where the great tadpoles swim.

There are possibilities all the way to the end;
whatever you do, take fishing with you.

The sound of air bubbles and that of lips
pursed just below the surface of an idea,
ready to bite, the bobber being pulled
down into the luminous murky world
of the imagination. Once airborne and
arcing the tiny mullet changing into the
giant orca right before our very eyes—

now that is something to keep.

CHARM

The two of them,
standing on the other side
of the airport window,
Mama wiping her eyes
and looking through her purse
for anything of hers
to lastly give.
Daddy, hands
one hundred leagues deep
in his salty pockets,
his black pearls
already secretly handed over
earlier in the day.
The way they stand there
with nowhere else
to go or be,
two watch lights watching,
until the last of me
is all the way out of sight.
Nobody waits like this anymore,
Nobody loves this way anymore.

Circle is never broken.

—CASSANDRA WILSON